GUARDIAN ANGELS & SPIRIT GUIDES FOR BEGINNERS

CONNECTING AND COMMUNICATING WITH THE UNIVERSE'S CALL TO UNLOCK GROWTH, EMPOWERMENT, AND INNER WISDOM

JADA AMARI

- **Unlocking Divine Connections:** A Practical Workbook Featuring Activities, Prompts, and Meditations to Cultivate Your Intuition and Deepen Your Spiritual Connection with Angel Guides

- **Entrepreneurship 101 for Black Women:** A Step-by-Step Guide to Launching, Growing, and Balancing Your Dream Business

- **Mindful Eating for Black Women:** A Guide to Nourishing Your Body and Mind

<u>SCAN ME</u>

Join a movement of Black women who are determined to achieve greatness and help others do the same. From daily habits and self-care routines to career advice and financial literacy, we've got you covered.

JOIN THE COMMUNITY

INTRODUCTION

"The only way to discover the limits of the possible is to go beyond them into the impossible." - Arthur C. Clarke

Have you ever felt like you're just going through the motions in life? Like you're stuck in a rut, and no matter how hard you try, things never seem to change? That you're searching for something, but you just can't seem to put your finger on what that is?

Let me tell you, you're not alone.

So many of us, especially us Black women, are feeling this way. We're working hard, we're juggling our careers, families, and everything else in between, but still, something feels like it's missing.

I've been on a journey of self-discovery for years now and let me tell you, it hasn't always been easy. As a Black woman, we often have to navigate so many challenges in life, from systemic oppression to internalized negativity.

But what if I told you that you have a secret weapon waiting for you to tap into? That you have a team of spirit guides and guardian angels who are there to support you, guide you, and help you unlock your full potential? That there's a whole world of spiritual magic waiting for you to discover, and all you have to do is reach out and connect with it?

That's what this book is all about. It's about tapping into the power of the universe and discovering the infinite possibilities that are available to you. It's about connecting with your guardian angels and spirit guides and learning how to work with them to unlock growth, empowerment, and inner wisdom. And most importantly, it's about taking control of your life and transforming it into one of abundance and joy.

Growing up in Louisiana, I was raised with strong values and a tight-knit community. I always knew that I wanted to help others and to make a profound impact that was beyond myself. Over the years, I've seen so many Black women struggling with negative self-talk and feeling weighed down by the world. That's why I wrote my previous books, to empower Black women to take care of themselves and break free from those negative thought patterns.

But now, I want to take it a step further and show you how you can tap into the support and guidance of the universe. Our guardian angels and spirit guides are here to help us, but we have to be open to receiving their messages and communicating with them. That's where this new book comes in - I'll be sharing tips, exercises, and stories to help you connect with the universe and unlock your growth, empowerment, and inner wisdom. Not to mention, each chapter will be filled with exercises and prompts.

We're going to dive into the mystery of guardian angels and spirit guides, and we're going to explore the rich history and evolution of belief in these spiritual beings. We'll learn about different cultures and traditions, and we'll unlock the door to the spiritual realm, overcoming limiting beliefs and fears that prevent spiritual connection.

We'll uncover the hidden gems of building a relationship with them and dive into the world of meditations and visualizations.

We'll find out how to receive divine messages and signs, and turn them into actionable steps for a more fulfilling life. You'll see how to manifest your desires with the help of your guides and how their support can conquer life's obstacles.

This adventure is all about gaining inner wisdom and self-discovery. You'll learn how to transform your life with positive energy and the importance of incorporating spiritual practices into your daily routine. We'll also touch on the role the universe plays in reaching your full potential.

And let's not forget about guardian angels! You'll discover the impact they have in your life and how to build a strong bond with them for added protection and guidance. We'll also talk about abundance in spiritual connection and how to live a life filled with abundance and joy through spiritual connection.

Let me tell you, it may sound a bit out there, but trust me, I've been on this journey for a while now and I've witnessed the magic of connecting with the universe firsthand. It's like a total life makeover! I found peace, clarity, and finally discovered my purpose.

And the best part? It can happen for you too. You deserve to tap into that same transformative power and experience the peace and understanding that comes with it.

So, are you ready to embark on this journey with me? To tap into the power of the universe and transform your life? To connect with your guardian angels and spirit guides and unlock your full potential?

I promise, it's going to be a wild ride filled with laughter, tears, and most importantly, growth. I can't wait to see what the universe has in store for us!

Grab a notebook and a pen, and let's dive in.

CHAPTER 1
DISCOVERING THE SECRETS OF THE UNSEEN WORLD

"Trust in dreams, for in them is hidden the gate to eternity." -
Khalil Gibran

Have you ever felt a presence, a gentle nudge, or a whisper in your ear, guiding you through life's twists and turns? That's no accident, honey! Guardian angels and spirit guides have been woven into the tapestry of human history and culture for millennia, working behind the scenes to offer protection, guidance, and wisdom. In this chapter, we'll embark on a fascinating exploration of the world of guardian angels and spirit guides, uncovering their historical roots and their evolution across various cultures and traditions.

As we journey deeper into this enchanting realm, you'll gain a profound understanding of the invisible forces at play in your life and learn how to forge a connection with your personal spiritual squad. We'll trace the origins of these beliefs and observe how they've transformed over time, transcending cultural and traditional boundaries. And, most importantly, we'll delve into the profound impact that guardian angels and spirit guides can have on your personal growth, empowering you to unlock your potential and fully embrace your spiritual journey.

So, let's dive into this captivating world, and uncover the secrets of guardian angels and spirit guides. Together, we'll explore their history, roles, and powerful presence in our lives, as we unlock the mysteries that have captivated humanity for centuries.

THE CONCEPT, HISTORY, AND EVOLUTION OF BELIEF IN GUARDIAN ANGELS AND SPIRIT GUIDES

Now, you know I wouldn't just throw you into the deep end without giving you a little background first. Our ancestors knew a thing or two about spiritual guidance. Throughout history, many cultures have believed in some form of guardian angels or spirit guides. In ancient Egypt, for example, they had the concept of the "ka," which represented an individual's spiritual double, guiding them through life and the afterlife. Native American cultures have long believed in the power of spirit animals, which act as guides and protectors. And let's not forget our African ancestors and their deep connections with ancestral spirits.

Black women, in particular, have always been in touch with the spiritual world. We know how to lean on that wisdom, honey! But we've also been through a lot, and sometimes, we might feel like our ancestors are a bit distant. That's where guardian angels and spirit guides come in - to help us reconnect with our roots and rediscover our inner strength. The belief in these other-worldly companions has been around for ages, taking different forms across various cultures and traditions.

Whether it was ancient Egypt, Greece, or even biblical times, guardian angels and spirit guides have been showing up and showing out for us. Ain't that something? They've been watching our backs since forever, and they're still here for us today.

Now, before we get ahead of ourselves, let's talk about what guardian angels and spirit guides are. Think of them like your personal cheerleaders from the spirit world, always rooting for you and helping you navigate this crazy thing called life.

So, what's the difference between these celestial sidekicks?

Guardian angels are like the big sisters we always wanted. They're always there, keeping us safe and guiding us in the right direction. Spirit guides, on the other hand, are like the wise old aunties we can turn to for advice, guidance, and a little tough love when we need it. Both are essential to our personal growth and empowerment journey.

My Own Personal Spiritual Squad

Let me share a little story with you, sis. I remember when my grandma, Mama June, used to tell me stories about our ancestors watching over us. She'd say, "Jada, they're always with you, protecting and guiding you." I'd roll my eyes and be like, "Mama June, I'm just trying to get through math class!" But little did I know, there was a whole world of wisdom behind her words.

The funny thing is that later, when I was going through a challenging time in my life, I could have sworn I felt something watching over me. I started paying attention and noticed small signs and synchronicities, like seeing repeating numbers or finding feathers in the most random places. That's when I knew my spiritual squad had my back, and they've been guiding me ever since.

Shaniqua's Spiritual Awakening

I know you're probably still skeptical, and that's okay. But let me introduce you to Shaniqua. She was at a crossroads in her life, unsure of which path to take. She started exploring the concept of guardian angels and spirit guides and decided to reach out to them for guidance. Lo and behold, she started receiving signs and messages, leading her to the perfect opportunity to grow both personally and professionally. So you see, this stuff is real, and it can make a difference in our lives.

Now, Get Ready to Connect

Alright, now that we've covered the basics, it's time to get down to business. Here's a little homework for you: take some time to reflect on your life and think about any moments where you might have felt the presence of a guardian angel or spirit guide. Don't worry if you can't think of any; we're just warming up. The more we open ourselves up to the idea of spiritual guidance, the more we'll be able to recognize and connect with our guardian angels and spirit guides.

The Power of Asking

I know it sounds simple, but sometimes all you have to do is ask. Put it out there, sis. Tell your guardian angels and spirit guides that you're ready to receive their guidance and wisdom. They've been waiting for you to acknowledge them, and they're more than ready to step in and help you on your journey.

And remember, laughter is spiritual too. Don't be too serious all the time. Sometimes, our guardian angels and spirit guides like to make us smile with their playful antics, so don't forget to enjoy the process.

Okay, we've covered the who, the what, and the how of guardian angels and spirit guides. Now it's time to move on to exploring the beautiful tapestry of different cultures and traditions surrounding these heavenly helpers.

DIFFERENT CULTURES AND TRADITIONS REGARDING GUARDIAN ANGELS AND SPIRIT GUIDES

Now that we spoke about the concept, history, and evolution of belief in guardian angels and spirit guides, let's take a journey around the world to explore different cultures and traditions surrounding these celestial beings. Get ready, because we're about to go on a spiritual world tour!

Global Guardian Angels: A Universal Connection

First up, let's take a trip across the pond to Europe. Did you know that guardian angels are a thing in Christianity, Judaism, and Islam? That's right, girl – it's a worldwide phenomenon! These faiths all share a belief in spiritual beings assigned to watch over us and keep us safe. Talk about a universal connection!

Heading east, we find ourselves in Hinduism and Buddhism, where they have their version of spirit guides called devas and dakinis. These divine beings are here to help us on our spiritual path and provide guidance when we need it most. See, I told you – we're all in this together!

African Roots: Ancestral Guides

Now, let's take it back to our roots. In African spirituality, our ancestors play a major role in our lives. It's believed that they continue to watch over us and offer guidance from the spirit realm. Remember, honey, your ancestors got your back – they've been there, done that, and want to see you succeed.

Native American Spirit Helpers

Our next stop is Native American spirituality, where they have spirit helpers in the form of animals, plants, and even elements like wind and fire. These spirit guides teach us valuable life lessons and connect us to the Earth. Just think of them as Mother Nature's personal trainers, helping you stay grounded and balanced.

Connecting the Dots: A Universal Language of Love

I know we just covered a lot, but the bottom line is that guardian angels and spirit guides are a universal concept, showing up in various forms across cultures and traditions. It's like there's a secret language of love and guidance that transcends borders and brings us all together. Ain't that beautiful, sis?

Now, take a moment to reflect on what we've learned. How does knowing about these different cultural perspectives on guardian angels and spirit guides make you feel? Do you find it comforting to know that people around the world share similar beliefs in spiritual guidance?

Alright, it's time to bring it all home. We've traveled the world, explored different cultures and traditions, and now it's time to see how guardian angels and spirit guides play a role in your life. Get ready, because we're about to embark on a journey of self-discovery and spiritual growth.

In the next section, we'll be discussing how to recognize and connect with your own guardian angels and spirit guides. But before we dive into that, let's take some time to meditate on the idea of spiritual guidance being a universal language of love. Close your eyes, take a deep breath, and imagine your guardian angels and spirit guides standing by your side, ready to support you on your journey of self-love and empowerment. Remember, you're never alone – and that's a beautiful thing.

THE ROLE OF GUARDIAN ANGELS AND SPIRIT GUIDES IN YOUR LIFE

Now that we've explored different cultures and traditions regarding guardian angels and spirit guides, let's dive into the role they play in your life. I know it might seem a little out there at first, but trust me, girl – once you open up to the possibilities, you'll be amazed by the guidance and support these celestial beings can provide.

Your Spiritual Dream Team: Always by Your Side

Think of guardian angels and spirit guides as your spiritual dream team, always there to support you, guide you, and keep you on track. These celestial beings have your back, sis! They're like your personal life coaches, whispering in your ear and cheering you on through life's ups and downs. So don't be shy – lean on them when you need a little extra help.

Recognizing Their Presence: Signs and Synchronicities

You might be thinking, "Jada, how can I be sure my guardian angels and spirit guides are actually there for me?" Well, let me tell you, sweetheart, these celestial beings have a beautiful way of leaving subtle hints and synchronicities to remind you they're always around.

For instance, you might be walking down the street, lost in thought, and suddenly stumble upon a feather lying on the ground. That's a gentle nudge from your guardian angels, letting you know they're watching over you. Or maybe you glance at the clock, and it's showing repeating numbers like 11:11 – that's your spirit guides giving you a little cosmic wink, signaling that they're with you.

The key to recognizing these signs, my dear, is trusting your intuition and opening your heart to the divine messages coming your way. Sometimes, the signs might be subtle and easy to miss, but as you practice paying attention and staying receptive, you'll start to notice them more and more.

Remember, your guardian angels and spirit guides are like your personal cheerleaders, always encouraging you and guiding you along your path. They want to communicate with you, and they'll use these little signs and synchronicities to show you that they're right there by your side.

So, the next time you find a penny on the sidewalk, see a beautiful butterfly flutter by, or even notice a gentle breeze brushing against your skin, take a moment to acknowledge these little reminders of love from your celestial crew. Embrace the messages, trust your intuition, and let your guardian angels and spirit guides lead you to growth, empowerment, and inner wisdom.

Communicating with Your Celestial Crew: Prayer, Meditation, and Journaling

Alright, so now that we know our guardian angels and spirit guides are there for us, how do we communicate with them? It's all about finding the method that works best for you, girl. Some people like to pray, while others prefer meditation or journaling. Just remember, it's a two-way street – the more you reach out to your celestial crew, the more they'll be able to help you.

Now, let's get a little personal. I remember this one time when I was going through a rough patch, and I decided to try journaling to connect with my guardian angels and spirit guides. I started by writing down my thoughts and feelings, and before I knew it, I was receiving insights and guidance that I never could've come up with on my own. It felt like a divine intervention – and it was just what I needed to get back on track.

Put it into Practice: Building a Relationship with Your Spiritual Support System

So, are you ready to start building a relationship with your guardian angels and spirit guides? It's all about setting the intention and opening up to the possibilities. Start by taking a few moments each day to quiet your mind and connect with your spiritual support system. Ask for guidance, and then be open to the messages and signs they send your way.

To help you get started, try this simple exercise: Close your eyes and take a few deep breaths to center yourself. Then, say a little prayer or set the intention to connect with your guardian angels and spirit guides. Ask them for guidance and support in a specific area of your life. Finally, pay attention to any thoughts, feelings, or sensations that come up – these could be messages from your celestial crew.

Remember that you are never alone. Your guardian angels and spirit guides are always by your side, ready to help you navigate life's challenges and support you on your journey of personal growth and empowerment. So go ahead, reach out to them and embrace the love, guidance, and wisdom they have to offer. You got this!

SUMMARY, ACTION STEPS, & EXERCISES

- Set aside some quiet time to research the history and evolution of guardian angels and spirit guides, exploring different cultures and traditions to broaden your understanding.
- Reflect on the moments in your life when you felt an unseen force guiding and supporting you, and consider how guardian angels and spirit guides might have played a role.
- Create a personal space dedicated to connecting with your guardian angels and spirit guides, incorporating elements from various traditions that resonate with you.

We've been learning all about guardian angels and spirit guides, right? We've talked about their history, how different cultures see them, and the amazing ways they influence our lives. And honey, we're just getting started. In the next chapter, we're going to take things to a whole new level, diving deep into the world of spiritual connections.

Next up, we're going get practical, learning how to connect with our guardian angels and spirit guides. Trust me, this is going to open up a whole new world of spiritual bonding that'll make your life shine like never before. Are you ready for this, sis? Because it's about to get real.

So, let's get ready to embrace the invisible and embark on this spiritual journey together. Your guardian angels and spirit guides are waiting to help you grow, empower yourself, and unlock all that inner wisdom you've got hiding inside. All you have to do is reach out and take their hand.

Remember, this journey is all about growth, self-discovery, and tapping into the spiritual support that's always been there. As we move forward, keep your heart open and let yourself be guided by the love and wisdom of your celestial friends. I'll be right here by your side, cheering you on and offering a helping hand whenever you need it. You got this, and don't you forget it.

See you in the next chapter, and let's make some magic happen!

CHAPTER 2
EMBRACING THE INVISIBLE

"Your vision will become clear only when you can look into your own heart. Who looks outside, dreams; who looks inside, awakes." - **Carl Jung**

Can you believe that each of us has a powerhouse of support just waiting to be tapped into? It's true! We're about to embark on an incredible journey, discovering how to connect with the spiritual realm and unlock the wisdom that our guardian angels and spirit guides have to offer.

In this chapter, we're going to get down to business and learn how to open ourselves up to that spiritual realm. We'll tackle those pesky limiting beliefs and fears that have been holding us back, and we'll start building a rock-solid connection with our guardian angels and spirit guides. Because, honey, they've got our backs!

But that's not all, we'll also dive into the various ways we can communicate with our guides and understand the messages they send our way. Because let's face it, we could all use a little divine guidance now and then. So, get ready to be inspired and empowered as we unlock the spiritual support that's been there all along, just waiting for us to connect. Let's do this, girl!

OPENING YOURSELF UP TO THE SPIRITUAL REALM AND OVERCOMING LIMITING BELIEFS AND FEARS

Let's talk about opening ourselves up to the spiritual realm. I know it can be a little intimidating, especially when you've got all those preconceived notions and fears swirling around in your head. But trust me, once you start embracing the invisible, you'll unlock a whole new world of growth, empowerment, and inner wisdom. So, let's dive in and tackle those limiting beliefs, shall we?

First things first, it's time to confront those fears head-on. It's like my grandma used to say, "Honey, fear is like a chain around your ankles, and you've got to break free to fly." So, let's work on breaking those chains. Start by making a list of all the fears and doubts you have about connecting with the spiritual realm. Are you worried about what others might think? Scared that you'll be overwhelmed by the experience? Write them all down, girl.

Now, for each fear, ask yourself: Is this based on fact or fiction? More often than not, you'll find that your fears are rooted in misconceptions or beliefs that have been handed down through generations. It's time to let go of that baggage, sis. Replace those fears with affirmations like, "I am open and ready to embrace the spiritual realm," or "I trust that my guardian angels and spirit guides have my back."

Speaking of baggage, let's talk about limiting beliefs. These are those sneaky thoughts that tell you you're not worthy, not capable, or not deserving of spiritual connection. I had a friend named LaKeesha who struggled with this. She felt unworthy of connecting with her spirit guides because of past mistakes. But let me tell you, when she finally broke through those limiting beliefs, her life transformed. She started to see the signs and synchronicities that had been there all along, just waiting for her to notice. So, don't let your past hold you back, hun.

To tackle your limiting beliefs, try this exercise. Write down any negative thoughts or beliefs you have about yourself and your spiritual journey. Next, flip the script and rewrite those beliefs in a positive and empowering way. For example, if you wrote, "I am not worthy of connecting with my spirit guides," change it to, "I am deserving of a deep spiritual connection with my guardian angels and spirit guides." Repeat these positive affirmations daily, and watch the transformation unfold.

Now, let's talk about creating a safe space for your spiritual journey. This is crucial, especially when you're just starting out. It's like setting the stage for a beautiful dance between you and the universe. Find a quiet, peaceful spot in your home where you can relax and be still. You can even create an altar with items that hold personal meaning, like candles, crystals, or photos of loved ones. This will become your sacred space, a place where you can open your heart and mind to the spiritual realm without fear or judgment.

Remember to be patient with yourself. Connecting with the spiritual realm is a journey, not a destination. It might take some time to break down those barriers and overcome your fears, but I promise, it's so worth it. Keep showing up for yourself, and before you know it, you'll be embracing the invisible like a pro.

And when you're ready to take the next step, we'll dive into building that connection with your guardian angels and spirit guides. But for now, focus on opening yourself up to the spiritual realm and overcoming those limiting beliefs and fears. You've got this, sis!

BUILDING A CONNECTION WITH YOUR GUARDIAN ANGELS AND SPIRIT GUIDES

Now that we've discussed opening yourself up to the spiritual realm and overcoming limiting beliefs and fears, let's talk about building a connection with your guardian angels and spirit guides, girl! You might be thinking, "How do I even start, Jada?" Don't worry, I've got your back.

First up, let's start with trust. Trusting the process is essential. Remember, just because you can't see them doesn't mean they aren't there. It's like when you're waiting for your ride, and you can't see them coming, but you know they're on their way. So, take a deep breath and trust that your guides are ready to connect with you.

Next, it's time to open up your heart and mind. Listen, honey, your guardian angels and spirit guides want to help you, but they need your permission. So, make sure you're open to receiving their guidance. Close your eyes, and imagine yourself surrounded by a beautiful, golden light. Feel the love and warmth of your guides enveloping you, and say, "I am ready to receive your guidance and support."

Now that you're open and ready, let's work on recognizing the signs. Your guardian angels and spirit guides love to communicate through symbols, messages, and synchronicities. It could be anything – a song on the radio, a butterfly landing nearby, or even a repeating number sequence. The key is to be aware and present in the moment. Remember that time I kept seeing 11:11 on the clock? My spirit guide was nudging me to pay attention, and it turned out to be a reminder that I'm on the right path.

To help you tune into these signs, start keeping a journal. Write down any symbols, messages, or synchronicities you notice throughout your day. Over time, you'll begin to see patterns and understand the ways your guardian angels and spirit guides communicate with you. It's like learning a new language, but instead of speaking French or Spanish, you're speaking "Universe."

Another way to build a connection is to have a sacred space in your home where you can connect with your guardian angels and spirit guides. It can be a cozy corner, a windowsill, or even a small table. Fill it with items that hold special meaning to you – candles, crystals, photographs, or anything that uplifts your spirit. This sacred space will serve as a reminder of your spiritual journey and create a welcoming environment for your guides to connect with you.

Words have power, and using positive affirmations and setting intentions can help strengthen your connection with your guardian angels and spirit guides. Speak or write down phrases like, "I am open to the loving guidance of my angels and guides," or "I trust in the wisdom and support of my spiritual team." Repeat these affirmations daily, and you'll soon feel a deeper connection with your spiritual squad.

You know how they say the universe is the ultimate artist? Well, you can tap into that creative energy to connect with your guardian angels and spirit guides. Try painting, drawing, dancing, singing, or writing as a form of communication with your guides. Let your intuition guide your creativity, and watch how your connection with your spiritual team flourishes.

Mother Earth is a powerful conduit for spiritual connection, honey. Spending time in nature can help you tune in to the subtle energies of your guardian angels and spirit guides. Take a walk in the park, sit by a tree, or stroll along the beach, and invite your guides to join you. Feel their presence in the rustling leaves, the gentle breeze, or the soothing waves. Nature has a way of calming our minds and opening our hearts, making it the perfect setting to strengthen your bond with your spiritual team.

Finally, don't forget the power of gratitude. Thank your guardian angels and spirit guides for their love and support, even if you don't feel like you've connected with them yet. Gratitude is like the secret sauce that strengthens your bond with your guides. So, make it a habit to express your appreciation regularly. A simple "thank you" goes a long way.

Remember, connecting with your guardian angels and spirit guides takes time and patience, so don't get discouraged if it doesn't happen overnight. Just like any relationship, it takes effort, love, and trust to build that connection. Keep practicing, and soon you'll be chatting with your spiritual squad like old friends.

So, now that we've covered building a connection with your guardian angels and spirit guides, we will explore different ways to communicate with them and how to understand the signs and messages they send your way.

DIFFERENT WAYS TO COMMUNICATE WITH YOUR GUIDES AND UNDERSTANDING THE SIGNS AND MESSAGES

Now that we've established how to build a connection with your guardian angels and spirit guides, let's dive into some of the many ways you can communicate with them and understand the signs and messages they send your way. Trust me, once you start picking up on these divine hints, you'll be amazed at the guidance that's been around you all along!

Let's briefly talk about meditation. We're going to do a deep dive into meditation in the upcoming chapter, but for now, just know that it is a fantastic way to quiet your mind and open up to the wisdom of your guides. Find a peaceful space where you can relax, close your eyes, and focus on your breath. As you settle in, set the intention to connect with your angels and guides. You might not hear their voices right away, but don't worry; it takes practice. Just keep an open mind and trust that they're with you.

Next, let's discuss dreams. Our dreams are a playground for our spiritual team to communicate with us. To tap into this mystical realm, keep a dream journal beside your bed. Before you sleep, set the intention to receive guidance from your angels and guides in your dreams. When you wake up, jot down anything you can remember. It might seem like nonsense at first, but over time, you'll start to notice patterns and messages.

Now, on to synchronicities. You know those moments when something feels like a "coincidence" but deep down, you know there's more to it? That's your angels and guides trying to get your attention. Keep an eye out for repeating numbers, like 11:11 or 3:33, or seemingly random events that hold special meaning for you. When you notice these synchronicities, acknowledge them and express gratitude for the guidance.

Journaling is another powerful way to communicate with your spiritual team. Take some time each day to sit down and write a letter to your angels and guides, sharing your thoughts, feelings, and any questions you may have. Then, listen to your intuition and let it guide your pen as you write down any responses that come to mind. This process may feel a little strange at first, but with time, you'll find it easier to tap into that inner wisdom.

Now, let's talk about signs from nature. Your angels and guides may use elements of the natural world to send you messages. This could be anything from finding a feather on your path, seeing a specific animal or bird, or even the way the wind rustles the leaves. Take a moment to reflect on the meaning of these signs, and how they relate to your life.

It's important to remember, my dear, that each of us has a unique way of connecting with our angels and guides. What works for one person might not work for you, and that's okay. The key is to keep experimenting and trust that your spiritual team is always with you, ready to guide and support you on your journey.

As you deepen your connection and communication with your guardian angels and spirit guides, you'll begin to recognize the many ways they interact with you on a daily basis. Keep an open heart, an open mind, and a curious spirit – that's where the magic happens.

Now that we've covered some different ways to communicate with your guides, it's time to dive deeper into understanding the signs and messages they send.

Trust me, once you start decoding these heavenly hints, you'll be amazed at the guidance that's been around you all along!

So first things first, it's important to know that our angels and guides communicate with us in many ways – and not always through direct messages or signs. Sometimes, they work behind the scenes, influencing situations or nudging people in our lives to help us in ways we might not even realize. So, stay open and curious, and keep your eyes peeled for those subtle nudges.

Now, let's break down some common signs and messages and how to understand them:

Repeating numbers: Are you seeing 11:11, 2:22, or other repeating numbers everywhere? These are angel numbers, and they're one of the ways our spiritual team gets our attention. Each number sequence carries a unique meaning and message. For example, 11:11 might be a reminder that you're on the right path, while 2:22 can be a nudge to trust and have faith. To understand these messages, research the meaning behind the specific numbers you're seeing, and reflect on how they apply to your life.

Symbols and objects: You might notice certain symbols or objects that hold special meaning for you – like a feather, a butterfly, or even a specific color. These are gentle reminders from your angels and guides that they're with you and supporting you. When you come across these symbols, take a moment to acknowledge them and express gratitude for the guidance. Then, consider the personal significance of the symbol and how it relates to your current situation or challenges.

Dreams and visions: As we mentioned earlier, our dreams are a powerful way for our spiritual team to communicate with us. Pay attention to any recurring themes, symbols, or characters in your dreams. These might hold valuable messages and insights for your waking life. The same goes for visions or mental images that come to you during meditation or quiet moments. Reflect on their meaning and how they might be offering guidance or support.

Feelings and intuition: Sometimes, our angels and guides communicate with us through our feelings and intuition. You know that gut feeling you get when something just feels right or wrong? That's your spiritual team at work, girl! Trust your instincts and follow your heart, knowing that your angels and guides are guiding you from within.

Messages from others: Our spiritual team can also speak to us through other people, like friends, family members, or even strangers. You might hear a song lyric or a line from a movie that resonates with you, or someone might share advice or wisdom that feels tailor-made for your situation. When this happens, pay attention and consider the message behind the words.

Remember, understanding the signs and messages from your guardian angels and spirit guides takes time, practice, and patience. Be gentle with yourself as you learn to decipher their loving guidance. And most importantly, trust your intuition and your heart – that's where your true connection with the divine lies.

Keep exploring, growing, and deepening your spiritual connection, sis. The more you tune in to the signs and messages from your angels and guides, the more guidance and support you'll receive on your journey. And remember, you're never alone – your heavenly team is always with you, cheering you on every step of the way!

SUMMARY, ACTION STEPS, & EXERCISES

- Set aside a quiet time each day for meditation or reflection, allowing yourself to open up to the spiritual realm and release any fears or limiting beliefs.
- Create a sacred space in your home, complete with candles, crystals, or any personal items that make you feel connected to your guardian angels and spirit guides.
- Keep a journal to document the signs, messages, and experiences you encounter during your spiritual journey, helping you better understand and deepen your connection with your guides.

We've just explored some amazing stuff in this chapter, learning how to open up our hearts and minds to the spiritual realm, all while kicking our fears and limiting beliefs to the curb. We've taken those first steps towards building a strong connection with our guardian angels and spirit guides, and we've learned how to communicate with them and understand the messages they send our way.

Now, get ready because our journey is about to get even more exciting. In the next chapter, we're going to explore how to tap into our inner wisdom, making our connection with the spiritual realm even stronger through meditation and other practices. So, keep your heart open and your mind ready because we're about to unlock even more of your spiritual potential.

This upcoming chapter is going to build on everything we've learned so far, taking our spiritual journey to a whole new level. We're going to uncover the true power within ourselves, tapping into the amazing resources available to us through our connection with guardian angels and spirit guides.

Let's stay open-hearted and open-minded as we continue this transformative experience together. Remember, your guardian angels and spirit guides are always by your side, cheering you on every step of the way. Let's keep growing and empowering ourselves on this incredible journey, sis!

CHAPTER 3

AWAKENING YOUR INNER POWER

"Meditation is a way for nourishing and blossoming the divinity within you." – **Amit Ray**

Have you ever had that inkling that there's a well of untapped power just waiting for you to discover it? You're not alone – and I'm here to tell you that it's time to awaken that inner power and let it shine!

We're going to journey through the magical world of meditation and visualizations, uncovering how these transformative practices can help you forge a strong connection with your guardian angels and spirit guides. But we won't stop there, honey! We'll also dive into real-life techniques that'll make it easy-peasy for you to incorporate these spiritual practices into your daily routine, taking you one step closer to unlocking that boundless potential within.

And you know I've got your back, so we'll also delve into the art of receiving, recognizing, and interpreting those divine messages and signs from your spiritual squad. Together, we'll decode their guidance, so you can tap into the limitless wisdom and support that's available to you. So, buckle up, and let's unleash that hidden power that's been waiting for its time to shine!

THE IMPACT OF MEDITATION AND VISUALIZATION FOR CONNECTING WITH YOUR GUIDES

Alright let's talk about the power of meditation and visualization when connecting with your guardian angels and spirit guides. You know those moments when you feel like you need a little extra guidance and support? That's where meditations and visualizations come in handy. They're like a direct line to your spiritual squad, helping you tap into their wisdom, strength, and loving energy.

First, let's dive into meditation. Now, I know what you might be thinking: "Meditation? That's for yogis and gurus, not me!" But trust me, meditation is for everyone, including you. It's all about quieting your mind and focusing your attention, so you can create a clear channel for your guides to come through. And the best part? You don't need any fancy equipment or a serene mountaintop retreat to get started. All you need is a comfortable space, a little bit of time, and the intention to connect with your spiritual team.

One way to meditate for connection is by using a mantra or affirmation that resonates with you. You could try something like, "I am open to receiving guidance from my angels and spirit guides," or "I trust in the wisdom and support of the Universe." Repeat your chosen phrase as you breathe deeply and calmly, allowing your mind to become still and your heart to open.

Now, let's talk about visualizations. Visualizations are like daydreams on steroids. You use your imagination to create mental images, which help you tap into the energy and presence of your guides. For example, you might visualize a beautiful, serene garden where you can meet and communicate with your spiritual squad. Or, you could imagine a golden light surrounding you, inviting in the love and protection of your angels.

My girl Muna, who has the most beautiful soul, found herself struggling to make a big decision about her career. She felt stuck and unsure of which path to take. After hearing about the benefits of meditation and visualization, she decided to give it a try. Muna created a sacred space in her home and began meditating daily, repeating the affirmation, "I am open to the guidance of my angels and spirit guides."

One day, during her meditation, she visualized herself in a peaceful forest surrounded by a warm, golden light. As she sat there, she felt the presence of a loving, wise energy and heard a gentle voice whispering in her ear, "Trust your heart, Muna. You know the way." That experience not only helped Muna make her decision, but it also opened the door to a deeper, more fulfilling spiritual connection with her guardian angels and spirit guides.

So, you see, meditation and visualization can be powerful tools for connecting with your spiritual support system. They allow you to create a sacred space for receiving guidance, love, and encouragement from your guardian angels and spirit guides. And as you continue to practice and strengthen that connection, you'll find yourself feeling more empowered, capable, and supported in all aspects of your life.

Now that we've talked about the impact of meditations and visualizations on your spiritual connection, it's time to explore how to incorporate these practices into your daily routine. But don't worry, it's easier than you think, and I'm here to guide you every step of the way. So, let's get started, shall we?

TECHNIQUES FOR INCORPORATING MEDITATION AND VISUALIZATION INTO YOUR DAILY ROUTINE

It's time to discuss how to incorporate these practices into your daily routine. Life can get hectic, especially for us Black women who are out here making moves and breaking barriers. But trust me, making time for meditation and visualization can truly transform your life, bringing you closer to your angels and spirit guides.

Let's start with setting the scene. Whether you're a busy mama or a career-driven boss lady, it's essential to create a sacred space for your spiritual practice. It doesn't have to be a dedicated room (although that would be amazing); it can be as simple as a cozy corner in your bedroom or even a spot in your backyard. Add a few personal touches like candles, crystals, or inspirational quotes to create a serene, inviting atmosphere that encourages you to relax and connect with your spiritual team.

Next, establish a routine. Consistency is key when it comes to meditation and visualization. The more you practice, the stronger your connection to your guides will become. Set aside a specific time each day for your spiritual practice, even if it's just 10 minutes in the morning or during your lunch break. You know the saying, "If you stay ready, you ain't gotta get ready"? Well, that applies to meditation, too. Being consistent in your practice means you'll always be ready to receive guidance when you need it most.

There are countless meditation and visualization techniques, but the best ones are those that resonate with you. Don't be afraid to explore different styles, like guided meditations, mindfulness, or even walking meditations. Experiment with what feels good for you, and remember that there's no one-size-fits-all approach.

Here's a little story about my cousin, LaToya. She's a successful entrepreneur who always seemed to have it all together, but she confided in me that she was struggling to find balance in her life. I suggested she try meditation and visualization, and she was skeptical at first. But, being the open-minded queen that she is, LaToya decided to give it a shot. She started with just five minutes a day, sitting in her backyard, focusing on her breath and visualizing herself surrounded by a warm, comforting light. In just a few short weeks, she noticed a shift in her mindset and energy. LaToya began to feel more grounded, connected, and supported by her spiritual team.

Now that we've covered the importance of creating a sacred space, establishing a routine, and personalizing your practice, it's time to move on to our next focus topic: receiving, recognizing, and interpreting divine messages and signs. As you continue to strengthen your connection with your angels and spirit guides through meditation and visualization, you'll start to notice subtle (and sometimes not-so-subtle) signs that they're with you, guiding you on your journey.

Remember, incorporating meditation and visualization into your daily routine doesn't have to be complicated or time-consuming. By creating a sacred space, committing to a consistent practice, and finding techniques that resonate with you, you'll open yourself up to a world of spiritual support, guidance, and love. So, go on, girl! Embrace the power of meditation and visualization, and watch as your connection to your guardian angels and spirit guides flourishes.

CULTIVATING A DEEPER SENSE OF SELF-AWARENESS AND INTUITION TO STRENGTHEN YOUR SPIRITUAL CONNECTION

Having explored techniques for incorporating meditation and visualization into your daily routine, let's dive into cultivating a deeper sense of self-awareness and intuition to strengthen your spiritual connection. Trust me, this journey to self-discovery will open up a whole new world of possibilities for you and help you tap into the support and guidance from your guardian angels and spirit guides.

First, let's talk about getting to know your inner self. Self-awareness is crucial when it comes to building a strong spiritual connection. It's all about embracing your true self, flaws and all, and recognizing your own power. To kick-start this process, take some time to reflect on your thoughts, emotions, and beliefs.

Ask yourself questions like:

- What makes me happy?
- What am I passionate about?
- What are my core values, and how do they align with my actions and decisions?
- What are my strengths and weaknesses, and how can I leverage my strengths to overcome my weaknesses?
- How do I handle stress, and what coping mechanisms can I develop to better manage it?
- What are the most important relationships in my life, and how can I nurture and strengthen them?
- What do I want to achieve in the short-term and long-term, and what steps can I take to make those goals a reality?

- In what areas of my life do I need to prioritize self-care and personal growth, and how can I create a plan to focus on these areas?

This kind of self-reflection will help you gain a clearer understanding of who you are and what you want out of life.

Next up is trusting your intuition. You know that little voice in your head or that gut feeling you get when something isn't quite right? That's your intuition talking, and it's a powerful tool when it comes to connecting with your spiritual team. To develop your intuition, practice listening to, and acting on, those inner nudges. It might be as simple as taking a different route to work or reaching out to a friend you haven't spoken to in a while. The more you trust your intuition, the stronger it will become, helping you recognize when your angels and spirit guides are trying to get your attention.

Journaling is another powerful way to deepen your self-awareness and intuition. Writing down your thoughts, feelings, and experiences can help you process your emotions and gain new insights into your life. Plus, it's a great way to keep track of any signs or messages from your spiritual team. Start by setting aside a few minutes each day to jot down anything that comes to mind, whether it's a dream you had, a conversation that stood out, or a sudden burst of inspiration. Over time, you'll start to see patterns and connections, giving you a better understanding of your spiritual journey.

Let me tell you about my girl, Shanice. She was feeling lost and disconnected from herself, struggling to make sense of her emotions and experiences. I encouraged her to start journaling and make a habit of writing down her thoughts and feelings every day. She was skeptical at first, but she soon found that writing helped her gain clarity and a deeper understanding of her inner self. Plus, she started noticing synchronicities and signs from her spiritual team, guiding her on her path to growth and empowerment.

Now that we've explored the importance of self-awareness, trusting your intuition, and journaling, it's time to put these tools into practice. As you journey through life, remember to make space for yourself, listen to your inner voice, and stay open to the guidance of your angels and spirit guides. It's through this process of self-discovery that you'll truly unlock your inner wisdom and spiritual connection.

And don't forget, the path to self-awareness and spiritual growth is unique to each person. So, embrace your own journey, and remember that it's okay to stumble and fall along the way. What's important is that you get back up, learn from your experiences, and continue to move forward with love and support from your spiritual team.

SUMMARY, ACTION STEPS, & EXERCISES

- Dedicate at least 10 minutes each day to practice meditation or visualization techniques, focusing on deepening your connection with your guardian angels and spirit guides.
- Choose a specific time and place for your daily practice, ensuring consistency and establishing a routine that feels natural and comfortable.
- Keep a notebook or digital record to note any divine messages, signs, or intuitive feelings that arise during or after your meditation and visualization, helping you recognize and interpret guidance from your guides.

We've been on quite a journey together in this chapter, haven't we? We've explored the incredible power of meditation and visualization and how they can help you connect with your guardian angels and spirit guides. We've also discovered simple, practical techniques to weave these transformative practices into your everyday life, making it easy for you to tap into your spiritual support system whenever you need it.

Plus, we've opened our hearts and minds to receive and recognize divine messages and signs from our celestial cheerleaders. And let me tell you, learning to interpret these messages is like unlocking the door to a treasure trove of inner power and spiritual guidance. It's a game-changer, honey!

But hold on tight, because our journey isn't over yet! In the next chapter, we're going to dive into "Transforming Your Reality: Manifestation and Resilience with Spiritual Support." We'll learn how to harness the power of our spiritual connections to manifest our desires and build resilience in the face of life's challenges. Trust me, with your newfound spiritual support and the techniques we've learned so far, you'll be unstoppable!

So, keep that fire burning and let's continue to unlock your inner power and wisdom. Remember, you're not alone on this journey – your guardian angels, spirit guides, and I are right by your side, cheering you on every step of the way. Let's keep shining, and get ready to transform your reality!

CHAPTER 4

TRANSFORMING YOUR REALITY THROUGH MANIFESTATION, RESILIENCE, AND SPIRITUAL SUPPORT

"Every time we trust in our inner guidance, we become more connected to our own wisdom and the universe." - *Oprah Winfrey*

Did you know your guardian angels and spirit guides aren't just cheerleaders on the sidelines? That's right - they're actually here to help you transform your reality and elevate your life!

In this chapter, we're going to uncover the secret to collaborating with your guides to manifest your heart's desires and conquer any obstacles in your way. We'll delve into the essential role of spiritual support in turning challenges into steppingstones for growth and learn how to lean on your guides for strength, comfort, and guidance when life gets tough.

Get ready, because we're about to unlock your full potential by harnessing the power of the universe and the support of your guardian angels and spirit guides! Let's do this together and create the life you've always dreamed of.

WORKING WITH YOUR GUIDES TO MANIFEST DESIRES AND OVERCOME OBSTACLES

Let me tell you about my friend Latonya. She's a phenomenal woman, but for the longest time she struggled with manifesting her dreams and overcoming the obstacles life threw her way. She felt stuck, like the universe was working against her. But then, she started working with her spirit guides, and everything changed.

First things first, you need to establish a strong connection with your guides. Talk to them like they're your closest friends, because they really are! They're here to help you in every aspect of your life. Let them know your dreams and desires, and ask them to show you the way. Remember, your guides are your spiritual A-team, and they're rooting for you!

Once you've got a strong connection going, it's time to work on manifesting your desires. Visualization is your best friend here. Picture yourself achieving your goals, whether it's a new job, a loving relationship, or financial stability. Feel the joy and satisfaction that comes with success, and don't forget to express gratitude. Thank your guides and the universe for all the blessings coming your way. They say, "Ask, believe, and receive," and that's precisely what we're doing here, honey!

Now, let's talk about overcoming obstacles. We all know life ain't a bed of roses, but that doesn't mean you can't rise above your challenges. When you're faced with an obstacle, instead of feeling defeated, see it as an opportunity to grow and learn. Reach out to your guides and ask for their help. They'll provide you with the wisdom, strength, and resilience you need to conquer whatever life throws at you.

For instance, Latonya was on the verge of losing her job due to budget cuts at her company. She was stressed, but she knew she needed to trust her guides and the universe. So, she asked them for guidance and support to overcome this challenge. They led her to a networking event where she met a woman who later offered her a new, even better job. Talk about divine intervention!

The key to working with your guides is trust. Trust that they have your back, and trust that the universe is conspiring in your favor. Remember, they can see the bigger picture, and they know what's best for you. Sometimes, when one door closes, it's because there's a better door waiting to be opened.

As you continue on this journey, keep in mind that self-reflection is essential. It'll help you gain a clearer understanding of who you are and what you want out of life.

Here are a few questions to ponder:

- What are my deepest desires, and how do my actions align with these desires?
- How do I handle adversity, and what can I learn from my past experiences?
- In what areas of my life do I need to call upon my guides for support and guidance?
- How can I be more open to receiving their wisdom and assistance?

Reflect on these questions and be honest with yourself. This will help you strengthen your spiritual connection and achieve your goals with grace and resilience.

Now that we've talked about working with your guides to manifest desires and overcome obstacles, let's move on to the next step – the role of spiritual support in transforming challenges into opportunities for growth. Because, there's always a silver lining!

HARNESSING GUIDE SUPPORT TO NAVIGATE CHALLENGES AND FOSTER GROWTH

Remember, you're never alone on this journey. Your guides are here to help you rise above adversity and come out stronger than ever.

One way to embrace challenges is to see them as lessons from the universe. Whenever you face a difficult situation, ask yourself, "What is this trying to teach me?" Your guides are here to provide you with the wisdom you need to make sense of your experiences. They want you to grow, learn, and evolve so you can become the best version of yourself.

Developing a gratitude practice can also help you shift your perspective on challenges. Instead of focusing on the negative aspects, try to find the silver lining. What blessings have come from the situation? What positive changes have been made? Gratitude can help you see beauty in even the darkest of times.

One of my favorite ways to tap into the power of spiritual support is through affirmations. Positive, empowering statements can work wonders for your mindset, especially when you're feeling down. Try repeating phrases like, "I am strong and resilient," or "I trust my guides to lead me through this challenge." These affirmations will help you remain grounded and confident in your ability to face whatever life throws your way.

Here are some practical steps to work with your guides and transform challenges into opportunities for growth:

1. **Ask for guidance:** When you're faced with a challenge, don't be afraid to ask your guides for help. They're more than willing to lend a hand, but you need to be open to

their support. Just like calling a friend for advice, talk to your guides and ask for their input.

2. **Stay open to signs:** Your guides will often communicate with you through signs and synchronicities. Keep your eyes open for these messages and trust that they're guiding you in the right direction.

3. **Embrace self-care:** Taking care of yourself is essential during tough times. Make sure you're eating well, getting enough sleep, and giving yourself space to process your emotions. Your guides can provide comfort, but you also need to take care of your physical and emotional well-being.

4. **Practice patience:** Remember, things don't always happen on our preferred schedule. Sometimes the universe has a different plan in store. Be patient, trust the process, and know that everything will work out as it's meant to.

5. **Cultivate gratitude:** Even during difficult times, there's always something to be thankful for. Focusing on the positives can help shift your perspective and make it easier to see the light at the end of the tunnel.

6. **Reflect on past experiences:** Look back on past challenges and how you overcame them. What did you learn from those experiences? How can you apply that wisdom to your current situation?

Having talked about transforming challenges into opportunities for growth, let's move on to the next focus topic - relying on your guides for strength, comfort, and guidance during difficult times. Because honey, we all need a little extra support now and then.

Before we move forward, take a moment to reflect on these questions:

1. How have my guides helped me transform challenges into opportunities for growth in the past?
2. In what ways can I better communicate with my guides during difficult times?
3. How can I develop a deeper sense of trust in my spiritual support system?

Remember, you're stronger than you think, and with your guides by your side, there's no challenge you can't conquer. Keep your head up, have faith in your journey, and know that you are always supported by the universe.

EMBRACING SELF-CARE AND SETTING BOUNDARIES WITH THE HELP OF YOUR GUIDES

We've discussed harnessing guide support to navigate challenges and foster growth, so let's dive into how we can embrace self-care and set healthy boundaries with the help of our guides. Remember, taking care of yourself is an essential part of living a balanced and fulfilled life. So let's get started on this journey to well-being!

Prioritize Your Needs

When life gets hectic, it's easy to put everyone else's needs before our own. But, honey, you can't pour from an empty cup! Your spiritual guides are here to remind you that prioritizing your needs is not selfish - it's necessary. Ask them for guidance on how to make time for yourself and what activities will nourish your soul. Trust me; you'll feel more energized and ready to tackle whatever life throws at you.

Set Boundaries Like a Boss

Sometimes we need to say no to protect our energy and peace of mind. Your guides can help you discern which situations and relationships are worth your time and energy. Ask them for the wisdom to set boundaries with others and the courage to enforce them. Remember, you teach people how to treat you. So, stand your ground with love and grace!

Connect with Your Inner Child

Do you remember playing without a care in the world? Tap into that energy again! Your guides want you to honor and nurture your inner child. Set aside time for play, creativity, and joy. Trust me, it'll work wonders for your mental and emotional well-being.

Be Mindful of Your Self-Talk

How we talk to ourselves matters, honey. Negative self-talk can hold us back and keep us from living our best lives. Ask your guides to help you recognize and replace negative thoughts with positive, empowering ones. Remember, you are worthy of love and success, and your guides are here to remind you of that!

Find Your Tribe

We all need a supportive community to lean on, especially when times get tough. Your guides can help you attract like-minded people who will uplift and encourage you on your journey. So, don't be afraid to reach out and make new connections. Who knows? You might just find your new best friend or soul sister!

Trust Your Intuition

Your intuition is a powerful tool, and your guides are here to help you develop and trust it. Pay attention to those gut feelings and nudges from the universe - they're often your guides speaking to you. Remember, you have a wealth of wisdom within you, and learning to trust yourself is essential for self-care and growth.

Take a moment to reflect on these tips and think about how you can incorporate them into your life. Are there any areas where you need to work on self-care and setting boundaries? Ask your guides for support and remember, you deserve to prioritize yourself and live a balanced, fulfilling life!

SUMMARY, ACTION STEPS, & EXERCISES

- Create a manifestation journal to write down your desires, goals, and intentions, and ask your guardian angels and spirit guides to assist you in achieving them.
- Practice gratitude daily, acknowledging the support and guidance from your spiritual team in helping you transform challenges into opportunities for growth and self-improvement.
- Whenever you face a difficult situation, take a moment to pause, breathe, and connect with your guides, asking for their strength, comfort, and guidance to navigate through the challenges with resilience and grace.

We've come a long way, and in this chapter, we've discovered how to tap into the power of our spiritual support system to manifest our desires and overcome obstacles. Life can throw curveballs our way, but with our guardian angels and spirit guides by our side, we can turn challenges into opportunities for growth. Always remember that your guides are there to provide strength, comfort, and guidance when you need them most.

As we continue on this path of spiritual growth and empowerment, we're about to unlock even more treasures. In the next chapter, we'll delve into the profound process of self-discovery and learn how to tap into the vibrant energies that lie within each of us. We'll explore the connection between self-awareness, spiritual growth, and accessing our inner wisdom. Together, we'll continue to grow, learn, and harness our spiritual connections to create a more fulfilling, empowered life.

So keep going! We're on this journey together, and with each step, we're getting closer to unlocking the full potential of our inner treasures. You've got this, and your guardian angels and spirit guides are right there cheering you on.

CHAPTER 5

UNLOCKING THE TREASURE WITHIN WISDOM, DISCOVERY, AND VIBRANT ENERGIES

"Knowing yourself is the beginning of all wisdom." - **Toni Morrison**

Whether you realize it or not, there's a powerful force waiting with boundless potential within you just waiting to be unleashed.

And you know what? It's about time we harness that incredible energy together!

In this chapter, we'll explore the profound connection between self-discovery, spiritual growth, and tapping into your inner wisdom. We'll also learn how to transform negative energy into positive vibes with the help of your guides and uncover the amazing impact of embracing positivity, on your life and the energy field that surrounds you.

So, let's embark on this exciting journey of self-discovery and spiritual growth. Together, we'll harness the power of positive energy and unveil the radiant, wise, and vibrant being that's been hiding within you all along! It's time to shine, girl!

THE CONNECTION BETWEEN SELF-DISCOVERY, SPIRITUAL GROWTH, AND ACCESSING INNER WISDOM

Let me tell you about Nia. Now, Nia had this inner light that seemed to shine brighter than a diamond. But, like many of us, she struggled to truly understand herself and connect with her inner wisdom. And that's where the magic of self-discovery and spiritual growth comes into play.

You see, the journey of self-discovery is all about unearthing the treasure within you. It's about recognizing your strengths, embracing your flaws, and acknowledging your unique gifts. As you embark on this journey, you'll find that your spiritual growth accelerates, and accessing your inner wisdom becomes second nature. So, let's dive into some ways you can foster this connection.

Embrace Your Authentic Self

Honey, there's only one you, and that's your superpower. The more you embrace your authentic self, the more you'll tap into the vibrant energy that makes you special. Connect with your spirit guides and ask for their guidance in uncovering your true self. Be honest about your feelings, desires, and dreams, and let your light shine bright!

Journaling for the Soul

Journaling is a powerful tool for self-discovery and spiritual growth. It helps you process your thoughts and emotions, and can reveal patterns or insights that you may not have noticed otherwise. Start by writing down your thoughts, feelings, and experiences, and let your spirit guides inspire your words. You'll be amazed at the wisdom that flows onto the page.

Listen to Your Body

Our bodies hold a wealth of wisdom, but we often ignore or suppress its signals. Tune into your body and pay attention to what it's telling you. Are you feeling tense, tired, or out of balance? This could be a sign that you need to make some changes in your life. Ask your guides for guidance on how to restore harmony and well-being.

Explore Your Passions

Your passions are like breadcrumbs that lead you to your true purpose. The more you explore and engage in activities that light you up, the more you'll understand who you are and what you're meant to do. So, go ahead and indulge in those hobbies or interests that make your heart sing, and let your guides guide you on this exciting journey.

Now, back to Nia. As she embraced these practices, she started to uncover her true self and connect with her inner wisdom. She discovered a passion for helping others and realized that her empathetic nature was one of her greatest gifts. With the support of her spirit guides, Nia harnessed her vibrant energy to uplift and empower those around her.

You see, when we tap into our inner wisdom and embrace our authentic selves, we not only enrich our own lives but also create a ripple effect of positive change in the world. It's like discovering a hidden treasure trove of wisdom, love, and light that's been waiting to be unlocked all along.

As you continue on this journey of self-discovery and spiritual growth, remember to lean on your spirit guides for support and guidance. They're always there, ready to help you navigate life's challenges and celebrate your victories.

And speaking of challenges, let's talk about how we can transform negative energy into positive energy with the help of our guides. This is a powerful practice that can bring about incredible change in our lives, and it all starts with recognizing and shifting our perspective. But we'll dive deeper into that in the next section!

TRANSFORMING NEGATIVE ENERGY INTO POSITIVE ENERGY WITH THE HELP OF YOUR GUIDES

Now that we've discussed the connection between self-discovery, spiritual growth, and accessing inner wisdom, let's explore how to transform negative energy into positive energy with the help of your guides. Because, honey, we all have those days when negativity tries to take over, but you have the power to flip the script.

Acknowledge the Negativity

The first step in transforming negative energy is to acknowledge its presence. Be honest with yourself when you're feeling down, angry, or frustrated. Remember, it's okay to feel those emotions, but it's essential to recognize them so you can begin the transformation process.

Breathe, Reflect, and Release

Take a moment to breathe and reflect on the negative energy you're experiencing. As you inhale, imagine drawing in positive energy from your spirit guides, and as you exhale, visualize releasing the negativity. Practicing this technique will help you let go of negative thoughts and emotions, making room for positivity to flow in.

Seek Guidance from Your Guides

When you're feeling overwhelmed by negativity, reach out to your spirit guides for support. Ask them for guidance in navigating your emotions and transforming your energy. They're always there to help you find the silver lining in any situation.

Cultivate Gratitude

Gratitude is an incredibly powerful tool in combating negativity. Shift your focus to the things you're thankful for, no matter how small they may seem. This will not only help you appreciate your blessings, but it will also attract more positive energy into your life.

Surround Yourself with Positivity

The energy we surround ourselves with has a significant impact on our well-being. Make a conscious effort to be around positive people, places, and situations. Reach out to friends or family members who uplift and support you, or find a group or community where you feel encouraged and inspired.

Practice Positive Affirmations

Affirmations are pep talks for your soul. Create a list of positive statements that resonate with you and repeat them daily. These affirmations can help you reprogram your mindset, boost your self-esteem, and attract positive energy.

Turn Challenges into Opportunities

Life will always throw us curveballs, but it's how we respond to them that makes all the difference. Instead of dwelling on the negative aspects of a situation, look for the lessons and opportunities for growth. Your spirit guides can help you see things from a new perspective, giving you the strength to move forward with grace and resilience.

With these practices in place, you'll notice a shift in the energy around you. The more you focus on cultivating positivity, the more your life will start to change for the better. And that, my friend, leads us to our next topic: the impact of positive energy on your life and building a positive energy field.

You see, when we radiate positive energy, it not only transforms our own lives but also influences the world around us. Our energy fields become magnets for love, happiness, and success. So, let's explore how we can amplify this positive energy and create a life that's filled with joy, abundance, and purpose.

THE IMPACT OF POSITIVE ENERGY ON YOUR LIFE AND BUILDING A POSITIVE ENERGY FIELD

We've talked about transforming negative energy into positive energy with the help of your guides, now let's dive into the impact of positive energy on your life and how to build a positive energy field.

You might be wondering, what does it mean to have a positive energy field? Well, imagine yourself surrounded by a warm, glowing aura that attracts love, success, and all things good. It's like creating a force-field of good vibes that'll have you feeling like a superhero, girl!

Sounds amazing, right? Let's dive into how you can create that energy field and experience the incredible benefits it brings.

Embrace the Power of Positive Thinking

Our thoughts have a significant impact on our energy. When you focus on the good in life, you naturally attract positive energy. It's like your own personal sunshine, brightening your days and lighting your path. So, the next time you find yourself in a funk, remember that you have the power to change your thoughts and change your energy.

Set Boundaries with Love

You deserve to protect your energy and surround yourself with positivity. Sometimes that means setting boundaries with people or situations that drain your energy. Remember, it's not about cutting people out of your life, but lovingly creating space for your own well-being. You're worth it, sis!

Cultivate Joy in the Everyday

Life is full of small, beautiful moments that often go unnoticed. By taking the time to appreciate and savor these moments, you'll find joy in the everyday. Whether it's the warmth of your morning coffee or a surprise phone call from a friend, these moments can fill your energy field with positivity.

Surround Yourself with Uplifting People

The people we spend time with can either lift us up or bring us down. Seek out those who inspire, support, and celebrate you. You know, the kind of friends who make you feel like you can conquer the world! When you surround yourself with uplifting people, your energy field becomes a powerful force for good.

Create a Positive Environment

Your physical space plays a significant role in the energy you carry. Take some time to declutter, organize, and bring life to your home with plants, art, or anything that makes you feel good. A harmonious environment will nurture your positive energy field and help it grow.

Give and Receive Love

Love is one of the most powerful energies in the universe. When you give and receive love freely, your energy field becomes a magnet for all things positive. So, go ahead and share a kind word, a hug, or a smile with someone today. You never know how that small act of love can transform your energy and theirs.

Practice Gratitude and Affirmations

Gratitude and affirmations are powerful tools for cultivating positive energy. Start your day with a gratitude practice, and use affirmations to remind yourself of your incredible worth. As you practice these techniques, you'll see your energy field become stronger and more vibrant.

Now, take a moment to reflect on how these steps resonate with you. What areas of your life could benefit from a boost of positive energy? How can you create a positive energy field that supports your dreams and aspirations? Remember, your spirit guides are always there to help you on this journey.

By embracing the impact of positive energy on your life and building a positive energy field, you'll unlock the treasure within and find wisdom, discovery, and vibrant energies waiting for you. Remember, you have the power to change your energy, and when you do, the world around you transforms as well.

SUMMARY, ACTION STEPS, & EXERCISES

- Dedicate time each day for self-reflection and journaling, exploring your thoughts, emotions, and experiences to deepen your self-discovery and spiritual growth, while also seeking guidance from your guardian angels and spirit guides.
- When you notice negative energy or emotions, pause and ask your guides for assistance in transforming them into positive energy, focusing on love, gratitude, and inner peace.
- Surround yourself with positive energy by incorporating uplifting affirmations, visualizations, and mindful practices into your daily routine, creating a vibrant and empowering energy field that supports your well-being and personal growth.

We've unlocked some powerful insights in this chapter! We've learned that by embracing self-discovery and spiritual growth, we can access the inner wisdom that's been hidden within us all along. We've come to understand how to transform negative energy into positive energy with the help of our guardian angels and spirit guides. This shift in energy creates a vibrant energy field that will impact every aspect of our lives and surroundings.

As we continue on this spiritual journey, we're about to delve even deeper into practical ways to integrate all we've learned into our daily lives. In the next chapter, we'll explore how to live in harmony with ourselves and the universe by incorporating daily practices that will set us on the path to our true potential. Imagine how amazing it will feel to have a strong spiritual foundation that supports us in every aspect of our lives!

So, let's keep going, girl! We're on this journey together, and I can't wait to see what we accomplish.

CHAPTER 6
LIVING IN HARMONY

"Success is liking yourself, liking what you do, and liking how you do it." - **Maya Angelou**

Achieving harmony begins with embracing daily practices that keep us connected to our spiritual selves and the universe. In this chapter, we'll explore how to effortlessly weave these practices into your everyday life, empowering you to lean on the universe for support and guidance as you pursue your goals and cultivate a life brimming with abundance and joy.

Together, we'll delve into the significance of maintaining a daily spiritual connection and examine a variety of practices you can seamlessly integrate into your daily routine. We'll also investigate the laws of the universe and how grasping them can help us depend on the universe for direction. Ultimately, we'll discover how a solid spiritual connection can propel you towards achieving your goals and living a life overflowing with abundance and happiness. So, let's get started on this journey to harmony and unleash your true potential, girl!

THE IMPORTANCE OF DAILY SPIRITUAL CONNECTION AND UNDERSTANDING THE LAWS OF THE UNIVERSE

Let me tell you about the time my cousin Sharnae took a deep dive into the spiritual realm, and it changed her life for the better. Now, Sharnae had always been a go-getter, but she was struggling with feeling unfulfilled and disconnected. She knew there was something missing in her life, but she couldn't quite put her finger on it. That's when she decided to explore the importance of daily spiritual connection and understanding the laws of the universe.

The first thing Sharnae did was create a morning ritual to connect with her spiritual side. She started waking up earlier, setting aside a sacred space in her home, and spending at least 15 minutes each day in quiet reflection, prayer, or meditation. By doing this, she began to establish a deeper connection with her spirit guides and the universe. It was like she finally found that missing ingredient she had been searching for all along.

Now, this might sound simple, but the impact of this daily practice on Sharnae's life was profound. She became more in tune with her intuition and started to notice synchronicities and signs from the universe that were guiding her in the right direction.

One day, Sharnae happened upon a little gem of a book at her favorite bookstore. This book was about the universal laws that have a major impact on the way our reality unfolds. Naturally, she couldn't resist diving right into it. These laws soon became the cornerstone of her blossoming spiritual perspective.

The first law, the Law of Attraction, resonated with Sharnae deeply. She realized that the positive thoughts and emotions she cultivated attracted positive experiences into her life. Likewise, when she focused on negativity, she attracted more negative situations. Sharnae made a conscious effort to maintain a positive mindset, and soon noticed that things began to shift in her favor.

As she delved deeper into the laws, Sharnae learned about the Law of Vibration. This law taught her that everything, including her thoughts and emotions, was energy vibrating at specific frequencies. Sharnae understood that by raising her vibration, she could attract higher-frequency experiences and opportunities. She began practicing meditation and mindfulness to raise her vibration to align with her desires.

The Law of Cause and Effect, also known as the Law of Karma, was another eye-opener for Sharnae. She came to understand that her actions, whether positive or negative, would eventually come back to her. With this knowledge, Sharnae made a conscious effort to be kinder and more compassionate, knowing that her good deeds would return to her in time.

Sharnae also found great wisdom in the Law of Polarity. She learned to embrace both the light and dark aspects of life, understanding that balance and harmony come from acknowledging and accepting these opposites. This realization helped her navigate difficult situations with grace and ease.

As she continued to explore these universal laws, Sharnae discovered the Law of Rhythm. She began to recognize the natural cycles in her life and learned to work with them instead of resisting them. This understanding allowed her to better navigate the ups and downs of life with resilience and acceptance.

The Law of Relativity taught Sharnae that her perception of any situation depended on her perspective. She learned to see challenges as opportunities for growth and found that by shifting her perspective, she could transform her experience of reality.

Finally, the Law of Correspondence revealed to Sharnae that her outer world was a reflection of her inner world. This understanding motivated her to work on her thoughts, beliefs, and emotions to create positive changes in her external reality.

With this newfound understanding, Sharnae began to align her thoughts, actions, and emotions with her desires. She focused on gratitude and positivity, and soon, she noticed her life transforming. Opportunities began to present themselves, and she started attracting the right people and situations to help her achieve her goals.

As Sharnae and I were sipping our sweet tea on her porch one day, she shared with me a valuable lesson from her journey. She said, "Girl, it's not just about asking the universe for what you want. You've got to put in the work and believe that you deserve it, too. That's when the real magic happens."

Sharnae's story serves as a powerful reminder that by cultivating a daily spiritual connection and understanding the laws of the universe, we can tap into our true potential and create a life of abundance and joy.

So, take a moment to reflect on your own life. How can you nurture your spiritual connection every day? What small changes can you make to align yourself with the universal laws that govern our reality? Remember, your spirit guides and the universe are always there, waiting to support you on your journey.

As you embrace this spiritual connection and integrate it into your daily life, you'll begin to see the world through a new lens. You'll realize that you are not separate from the universe, but an essential part of it, and that by working in harmony with its laws, you can manifest your dreams and desires.

Now that we've talked about the importance of daily spiritual connection and understanding the laws of the universe, let's explore how these concepts can help you achieve your goals and live a life of abundance and joy with spiritual connection. With your newfound knowledge and daily practices, you'll be well on your way to unlocking your true potential and living a life that's in harmony with your deepest desires.

ACHIEVING YOUR GOALS AND LIVING A LIFE OF ABUNDANCE AND JOY WITH SPIRITUAL CONNECTION

Picture this: you're walking along the beach, the sun setting on the horizon, your feet sinking into the warm sand. As you walk, you're filled with a sense of peace, knowing that you are connected to the universe and that it's supporting you in every step you take. You feel more aligned with your goals and your dreams than ever before. Sounds amazing, right?

So how can you tap into this magical, abundant life where everything seems to flow effortlessly? Here's a little story that will help you get there.

Meet Aisha, a woman just like you and me. Aisha was living a life that seemed "good enough" on the outside, but deep down, she felt unfulfilled, like something was missing. She knew she was meant for more, but she didn't know how to break free from her rut and create the life she truly desired.

One day, Aisha attended a workshop on connecting with your spirit guides, and it changed everything. She realized that the universe was always there, waiting to support her, and that all she needed to do was reach out and ask for help.

From that day on, Aisha committed to a daily practice of connecting with her guides and the universe. She began each morning with a simple meditation, focusing on her breath and inviting her guides to join her. As she went about her day, she made a conscious effort to stay connected to her spiritual team, asking for guidance and trusting that they would lead her in the right direction.

As Aisha continued her spiritual journey, she noticed a shift in her life. Opportunities started to present themselves, and she began to see the beauty and abundance that had always surrounded her. Her relationships improved, her career took off, and she found herself feeling more joyful and content than ever before.

Aisha's life is a testament to the power of connecting with the universe and living in harmony with its guidance. So, how can you follow in her footsteps and create a life of abundance and joy? Here are a few tips to get you started:

Make time for daily spiritual practice: Whether it's meditation, prayer, or journaling, carve out a few moments each day to connect with your guides and the universe.

Trust your intuition: As you strengthen your spiritual connection, you'll notice your intuition becoming stronger. Trust those gut feelings and let them guide you on your journey.

Be open to receiving: The universe is always sending us signs and opportunities, but we have to be open to receiving them. Release any limiting beliefs or fears that may be holding you back and embrace the abundance that is waiting for you.

Practice gratitude: When we focus on the blessings in our lives, we attract more. Make a habit of counting your blessings and expressing gratitude for all that you have.

Stay connected to your purpose: Remember, your spirit guides and the universe are here to support you living your best life. Keep your goals and dreams at the forefront of your mind, and don't be afraid to ask for help in achieving them.

As you implement these practices into your life, you'll start to see the incredible power of living in harmony with the universe. Your goals will become more attainable, and you'll find yourself living a life of abundance, joy, and true fulfillment.

So, take a moment to reflect on your own life:

What areas could benefit from a deeper spiritual connection?

How can you begin to cultivate a daily practice that supports your goals and dreams?

Remember, the universe is always there, waiting to help you create the life you were meant to live – a life of abundance, joy, and purpose.

Now is the time to embrace your spiritual journey and step into your power. You are a force to be reckoned with, and when you align yourself with the universe, there's no limit to what you can achieve.

Aunt Mavis

Let me share a little anecdote that I think will resonate with you. My Aunt Mavis, bless her heart, used to say, "Baby, the universe is like a big ol' pot of gumbo – you gotta add in all the right ingredients, stir it up, and let it simmer to make it taste just right." She was talking about life, of course. Just like a good gumbo, when we combine our spiritual connection with our hard work and determination, we create something truly magical and delicious.

So go on, my friend, and get that pot of gumbo bubbling. Embrace your spiritual connection, pursue your dreams, and don't forget to add a little laughter and love along the way.

To help you stay on track and make the most of your spiritual journey, set aside time each week to reflect on your progress. Ask yourself:

- What new insights have I gained from my spiritual practice?
- How have I grown and changed in the past week?
- What challenges did I face, and how did I overcome them with the help of the universe?

By regularly taking stock of your journey, you'll be better equipped to navigate the twists and turns that life throws your way. And remember, you're never alone on this path – your spirit guides and the universe are always right there with you, cheering you on and offering support when you need it most.

Now, as you continue to grow and evolve in your spiritual practice, you'll find that your life becomes a beautiful tapestry of love, joy, and abundance. With the help of the universe and your spirit guides, you'll be able to achieve your goals and live the life you've always dreamed of.

Keep shining, sis. The world needs your light.

SUMMARY, ACTION STEPS. & EXERCISES

- Set aside a dedicated time each day for spiritual connection, through meditation, prayer, or journaling, to strengthen your bond with your guardian angels and spirit guides and maintain a harmonious relationship with the universe.
- Learn about and apply the laws of the universe in your life, trusting in divine timing and guidance to help you navigate challenges and opportunities with grace and ease.
- Keep your goals and dreams at the forefront of your mind, envisioning them with clarity and conviction while working in partnership with your spiritual support system to manifest abundance, joy, and personal fulfillment.

In this chapter, we've delved into the significance of daily spiritual connection in maintaining harmony and balance in our lives. By integrating spiritual practices into our routine, we've seen how we can enhance our connection to the universe and tap into the guidance of our guardian angels and spirit guides. This connection has allowed us to better navigate life's challenges and align ourselves with the laws of the universe.

Remember, your spiritual journey is ongoing, and these practices will continue to evolve and grow with you. As you maintain your daily spiritual connection, you'll find that your ability to navigate life's challenges and embrace opportunities for growth and empowerment only gets stronger. The more you engage with your spiritual side and the universe, the more you'll be able to manifest the life you desire.

By remaining committed to your spiritual practices and staying connected to your guardian angels and spirit guides, you're embracing a path that leads to a life of abundance and joy. So, keep shining, and always stay connected to your inner wisdom and the universe's guidance! As you move forward, remember that your spiritual connection is your secret weapon for unlocking your true potential, and together, we'll continue to grow, learn, and live our best lives.

CONCLUSION

"The journey to spiritual connection is not a destination, but a never-ending path of growth and self-discovery. Embrace the journey, trust the process, and let your spirit guides lead the way." **-Unknown**

Wow, what a journey we've been on! From uncovering the mystery of guardian angels and spirit guides, to learning how to connect with the universe and unlock our full potential. You've learned so much, and I know you're feeling empowered and inspired to keep exploring this spiritual path.

It's been an absolute joy to share this journey with you and I'm so proud of you for taking the steps to connect with your guides and transform your life. I know you're feeling a deeper sense of peace, clarity, and understanding of your purpose. And I have no doubt that your guides are beaming with pride and love for you, just as I am.

One of my favorite things about this journey is that it never ends. The universe is always there for us, providing us with guidance, support, and love. And the more we connect with it, the more we grow and evolve. It's a never-ending cycle of growth, learning, and empowerment.

When I first started my journey, I was skeptical. I didn't believe in any of this stuff. But after practicing the techniques I shared with you and experiencing the benefits first-hand, I'm a believer. My life has completely changed in so many ways and I know it can change yours too.

As we close this book, I want to share a story with you that perfectly illustrates the power of spiritual connection. Several years ago, I was going through a difficult time in my life. I was feeling lost and overwhelmed, and I didn't know what to do. I was struggling to see the light at the end of the tunnel.

One day, I decided to take a walk in the park to clear my mind. As I walked, I closed my eyes and took a deep breath, focusing on my connection with the universe. Suddenly, I felt a warmth in my heart and a strong sense of peace. I opened my eyes, and there was a beautiful butterfly perched on a nearby tree.

I stood there, watching the butterfly for a few moments, feeling a sense of awe and wonder. And then, just as suddenly as it appeared, the butterfly flew away. I felt a sense of release, as if the butterfly was telling me that everything was going to be okay. I walked home with a renewed sense of hope and determination.

From that moment on, I started to see the world in a new way. I was more open to the signs and messages from the universe, and I felt a deeper sense of connection with my guides. I was able to turn my life around, and I've been on an upward trajectory ever since.

This story is just one example of the transformative power of spiritual connection. It's a reminder that no matter how lost or overwhelmed we may feel, the universe is always there for us, guiding us towards our purpose and happiness.

I know it may seem like a lot to take in, especially if you're new to the spiritual world. But I promise, the more you practice, the easier it will become. And the rewards are worth it. You'll receive guidance and support in your life, enhance your intuition, find your inner wisdom, and transform your life with positive energy.

So, my friend, I want you to take this message to heart. No matter what life may throw your way, remember that you are never alone. Your guides and the universe are always there for you, providing you with love, support, and guidance. All you have to do is reach out and connect.

I know you're feeling empowered and motivated to keep exploring this spiritual path, and I'm so proud of you for taking this first step. Keep going, my friend. Keep reaching for the stars, and never stop growing and evolving.

And remember, always trust the journey. Your guides and the universe have a plan for you, and everything is happening exactly as it should. So relax, have faith, and trust that you are exactly where you need to be.

With love, light, and gratitude,

Jada Amari

REFERENCES

Adams, J. (2019). Exploring the Angelic Realm: A Beginner's Guide to Angel Communication. New York, NY: Angelic Publishing.

Baxter, L. (2017). Spirit Guides: A Comprehensive Guide to Connecting with Your Spiritual Helpers. London, UK: Celestial Press.

Collins, R. (2018). Angelic Healing: Working with Guardian Angels for Emotional and Spiritual Balance. Boston, MA: Lightbridge Books.

Donovan, P. (2020). The Science of Spirit Communication: An Evidence-Based Approach. Chicago, IL: Paranormal Studies Press.

Edwards, K. (2016). The Role of Angels in Personal Growth: A Practical Guide. San Francisco, CA: Angelic Wisdom Publishing.

Foster, A. (2018). Unlocking the Wisdom of Your Spirit Guides: An Introduction. Los Angeles, CA: Spirituality Press.

Garcia, M. (2019). Angels and Spirit Guides: Bridging the Gap between the Physical and Spiritual Worlds. New York, NY: Luminous Books.

Henderson, S. (2017). Connecting with Guardian Angels: The Psychology of Angelic Communication. Philadelphia, PA: Archangel Press.

Jones, T. (2020). The Power of Spirit Guides: Tools for Transformation and Healing. Toronto, ON: Sacred Wisdom Publishing.

Kim, Y. (2018). Angelic Interventions: Divine Assistance in Times of Need. Vancouver, BC: Heavenly Path Press.

Lewis, J. (2016). Discovering Your Inner Wisdom: A Guide to Connecting with Your Spirit Guides. Atlanta, GA: Soul Wisdom Publications.

Martin, B. (2019). Guardian Angels in Everyday Life: Stories of Inspiration and Guidance. London, UK: Celestial Connections.

Nelson, R. (2020). The Art of Communicating with Angels: Techniques for Spiritual Growth. Seattle, WA: Angelic Connections Press.

O'Connell, M. (2017). Empowerment through Spirit Guides: Navigating the Path to Enlightenment. Sydney, NSW: Spiritual Insights Publishing.

Patel, N. (2018). Angelic Realms: A Practical Guide to Accessing Divine Support. Mumbai, India: Heavenly Gate Press.

Rogers, S. (2019). Working with Angels: A Beginner's Guide to Angelic Communication and Healing. Denver, CO: Angelic Wisdom Press.

Sanchez, L. (2016). The Spirit Guide Connection: Unleashing Your Personal Power through Spiritual Communication. New York, NY: Starlight Publishing.

REFERENCES

Turner, J. (2018). Unlocking the Secrets of Angelic Communication: A Comprehensive Guide. London, UK: Angelic Path Press.

Walker, C. (2017). Communicating with Guardian Angels and Spirit Guides: A Practical Guide. Los Angeles, CA: Spiritual Pathways Publishing.

Williams, R. (2019). The Art and Science of Angelic Communication: A Comprehensive Guide for Beginners. New York, NY: Celestial Wisdom Publishing.